THE IMPACT OF TECHNOLOGY IN
SPORTS

Matt Anniss

heinemann
raintree

To contact Capstone Global Library, please call 800-747-4992, or visit our web site www.capstonepub.com

Edited by James Benefield and Amanda Robbins
Designed by Steve Mead
Original illustrations © Capstone Global Library Ltd 2015
Picture research by Tracey Cummins
Production by Helen McCreath
Originated by Capstone Global Library Ltd
Printed and bound in China by RR Donnelley Asia

19 18 17 16 15
10 9 8 7 6 5 4 3 2 1

Library of Congress Cataloging-in-Publication Data
Cataloging-in-Publication Data is available at the Library of Congress website.

ISBN 978-1-4846-2636-8 (hardcover)
ISBN 978-1-4846-2641-2 (paperback)

This book has been officially leveled by using the F&P Text Level Gradient™ Leveling System.

Acknowledgments
Alamy: Agencja Fotograficzna Caro, 16; AP Photo: Damian Dovarganes, 14; Corbis: Andrew Richardson/Icon SMI, 39, Neil Tingle, 45, Sam Bagnall/AMA, 43; Getty Images: Action Plus, 28, Adam Nurkiewicz, 21 Middle, AFP/BEL-GAYORICK JANSENS, 21 Bottom Left, AFP/FRANCK FIFE, 30, AFP/OLIVIER MORIN, 27, Alex Livesey, Cover Bottom, Bryn Lennon, 17, BSIP/UIG, 9, 40, Cameron Spencer, 36, Christof Koepsel/Bongarts, 15, David Cannon, 34, Ian Walton, 5, 12, Julian Finney, 37, Lintao Zhang, 48, Lutz Bongarts/Bongarts, 33, MCT/Chuck Myers, 32; iStockphotos: filo, Cover Top Left, shapecharge, 6; Photoshot: Caro, 11; Science Source: Pascal Goetgheluck, 25; Shutterstock: 3d_kot, 31 Top, Alhovik, 31 Bottom, Cover Top Middle, Design Element, Dragan85, Design Element, michaeljung, 23, Mitch Gunn, 21 Bottom Right, Monkey Business Images, 21 Top, Natursports, Cover Top Right, Neale Cousland, 35, Pavel L Photo and Video, 47, Rob Marmion, 19, style_TTT, Design Element, Surrphoto, 42, Thinkstock: Photos.com, 13.

We would like to thank Dr. Michael Jenkins for his invaluable help in the preparation of this book.

007346RRDF15

CONTENTS

Some words are shown in bold, **like this**. You can find out what they mean by looking in the glossary.

1 CHANGING THE GAME THROUGH TECHNOLOGY

Some people think of sports as just contests between athletes. Races, games, and fights are decided by a combination of hard work, natural talent, and a desire to win. It's one-on-one or team-against-team, and the best athletes on the day will win, regardless of anything else.

In practice, it is not so simple. While the best athletes may cross the finish line first, their path to glory—like that of their competitors—is shaped by science and technology.

What is technology?

Technology can be defined as science or knowledge put into practice, in order to solve problems or create useful tools. Technology is constantly evolving, so what was seen as **revolutionary** just 5 or 10 years ago may now be out-of-date. Athletes must embrace the latest technology and scientific thinking to stay ahead of their competitors.

Improving performance

Almost every aspect of every sport you can think of has in some way been touched by technology:

- Better understanding of the way the human body works during exercise has helped scientists and coaches to create training plans. These help athletes get to the starting line in peak **physical** shape.
- Increased understanding of the role diet plays helps athletes eat the right things to fuel their efforts.
- Cutting-edge equipment for analyzing performance helps athletes train harder, for longer periods of time.
- Understanding scientific concepts such as aerodynamics has helped **manufacturers** to make equipment that moves more efficiently through the air.
- Clothing makers use the latest textile technology to create sportswear that helps athletes to record super-fast times.

Looking to the future

Sometimes, scientific and technological innovations even change the way a sport is played. For example:

- Tennis players with faster serves began to dominate the sport after lightweight rackets were introduced in the 1980s.

- Lightweight clubs had a similar impact on golf, allowing players such as Tiger Woods and Rory McIlroy to hit the ball straighter and farther. As a result, scores tumbled and many top courses were lengthened to make them more challenging for golfers.

Also, look at the sport of javelin throwing. In 1984, Uwe Hohn set a new world record of 344 feet (104.8 meters). The governing body of athletics responded by redesigning the javelin to guarantee shorter throws. In 2012, the men's gold medal at the Olympic Games was won by a throw of 277 feet (84.58 meters)—nearly 67 feet (20 meters) less than Hohn's 1984 record.

« Barbora Špotáková is the current female Olympic champion in javelin throwing. Technology has made the average javelin throw shorter.

2 TECHNOLOGY AND SPORTS TRAINING

Technology can be used to help athletes perform during big races and important games. But that wouldn't be possible without a lot of training beforehand. Put simply, you can't excel at sports if you don't get the right training.

How training works

How athletes train varies depending on their sport, but they all train according to the same basic principles. When you exercise regularly, your body makes certain physical **adaptations**. Depending on the type of exercise, your muscles could get leaner or bigger. Also, your heart will get stronger, to allow it to pump more blood around the body during workouts. Over time, these adaptations change your body and allow you to perform the same exercise for longer, or at a higher **intensity**.

>> Thanks to decades of scientific research, we now know how and why the body adapts to regular exercise.

THE SCIENCE BEHIND: HARDER, BETTER, FASTER, STRONGER

If you did not usually get much exercise and started jogging three times a week, you would find it difficult at first. You'd get out of breath quickly, you'd sweat a lot, and you'd find that you couldn't run very far without needing to rest.

But this would get better with time. After a few weeks of regular jogging, you'd find it easier to breathe during exercise and you'd be able to run farther, at a faster pace, before you had to stop. This is an example of your body adapting to the demands of training.

Regular training will:

- strengthen your heart, allowing it to pump blood to your muscles more efficiently
- make your muscles more resistant to **fatigue**
- change your lungs so that they can increase lung capacity more efficiently during exercise. This is important, as it allows more oxygen into the blood, which is then used to power your muscles.

Practice makes perfect

The adaptations don't stop there, either. If your chosen sport involves kicking, throwing, or any kind of repetitive muscle movement, you will improve through regular training. By practicing the skill enough, it becomes second nature.

Scientists have put this knowledge to good use. They have invented amazing training aids and computer systems to help athletes of all levels train "smarter."

PIONEERS

ARCHIBALD MACLAREN

Gym owner Archibald MacLaren took exercise seriously at a time when few people did. In 1867, he wrote a book in which he explained that regular exercise, with gradual increases in training, had major effects on the body. In the 20th century, scientific tests proved his theory to be correct. MacLaren also pointed out for the first time that regular exercise helped to reduce stress. Relieving stress cuts down the likelihood of getting illnesses such as cancer, stroke, and heart disease.

Fitness testing

Fitness is a way a person's physical condition is measured, including the person's capability to exercise regularly. A key part of sports training today is fitness testing. Through this, athletes can check whether their training plans are working and also what fitness potential they have. Fitness testing can also be used at the start of a new exercise program to measure **base fitness**. This makes sure that athletes don't do too much, too quickly.

TECHNOLOGY THROUGH TIME: THE SHUTTLE RUN

Before advances in technology, coaches would have to resort to timing laps of running tracks or swimming pools or to weight-lifting tests in gyms to monitor their athletes' progress. Another popular method, still used in some schools today, was the "shuttle run" (sometimes also called a multistage fitness test or beep test). This involves running 66 feet (20 meters), then back again, in time to a beeping sound. As the test progresses, the sounds get closer together, meaning you have to run faster. Now you can do your own test by downloading an application (app) for your smartphone.

Measuring movement

Over the last 20 years, computer technology has improved dramatically. This has affected the lives of athletes in many ways. For example, it has allowed scientists to invent amazing new ways to test and analyze almost every aspect of fitness.

Find your maximum

Isokinetic muscle testing is used to measure the strength of a group of muscles, usually around a joint, such as the knee or ankle. Athletes are strapped into a special machine, which controls their speed while they perform a movement, such as pedaling.

The machine is connected to a computer, which tracks the athlete's speed and torque (the force applied during the pedaling motion). This calculates the strength of the muscles used during the test.

Coaches can use this information to accurately design weight training programs, as well as to figure out a safe volume of training that reduces the risk of injury. **Isokinetic** muscle testing is regularly used to monitor athletes' progress when they are recovering from injuries.

CASE STUDY / VO$_2$ MAX TESTING

VO$_2$ max testing involves athletes running on a treadmill or sitting on an exercise bike while breathing into a mask. This mask is used to measure the volume of air expired (breathed out), along with the exact mixture of oxygen and carbon dioxide in the expired air. At the same time, the athlete is wired to a computer that monitors how fast his or her heart is beating (known as the "heart rate," and measured in beats per minute).

The measurements taken during VO$_2$ max testing tell athletes how much oxygen their body uses during exercise. If you know this, you can tailor your training so that you are pushing your body just enough to make the adaptations needed to get fitter.

⌃ VO$_2$ max testing is used to measure your heart rate and lung capacity during exercise. From this, you can figure out how far you can push your body during training.

Environment training

For **professional** athletes, it is important to train in the environmental conditions they will find when they actually compete. In particular, weather conditions can affect our ability to exercise. Heat, humidity, and air quality can all make exercising difficult.

- Heat: When you exercise in high temperatures, the heat makes you sweat more to try to cool your body down. Unless you replace the fluid lost through sweating (having frequent access to drinking water is important), you will become dehydrated. It gets harder to exercise and, in extreme circumstances, dehydration can seriously harm your body.
- Humidity: This is a measurement of how much water is in the air. On humid days, the increased level of moisture in the air makes it feel hotter. This, in turn, makes you feel warmer and stops your sweat from evaporating into the air. During exercise, this can make you dehydrate quicker.
- Air quality: As you get farther away from sea level, the amount of oxygen in the air around you decreases. The higher you go, the "thinner" the air is. That makes it more difficult to breathe. This is why exercising at high altitude—for example, at the top of a mountain—is so difficult. Other things can affect the quality of the air, too, such as pollution.

THE SCIENCE BEHIND: ALTITUDE TRAINING

Although exercising at high altitude is difficult, research has shown that it can be great for athletes. When they train at high altitude, athletes' bodies naturally adapt to the lack of oxygen in the air. Their bodies get better at delivering oxygen to the muscles. Then, when they race at sea level, athletes can perform better for longer periods of time. This is because their bodies use oxygen more efficiently.

High up, down low

The benefits of training at high altitudes have inspired scientists to find ways to re-create those conditions at sea level. Many athletes now use altitude chambers (sometimes called hypobaric chambers) in their training. These are special sealed rooms in which you can control the amount of oxygen in the air. These rooms make it seem like you are getting all the benefits from training on top of a mountain.

CASE STUDY / INDOOR SNOW CENTERS

Snowboarders and skiers require snow to practice their sports. In countries with few snow-covered mountains, Winter Olympians have to make do with **artificial** slopes made from matting and plastic bristles. Better still, they use high-tech indoor "snow domes," which keep the air up to a cool 23 degrees Fahrenheit (-5 degrees Celsius) and fire freshly made "snow" over hills and ramps. The snow is created using a special machine. This pumps a mist of water into the cold air inside the dome. The water droplets in the mist quickly turn into ice crystals, which gather together to form snow.

⌄ High-tech indoor snow centers re-create the conditions skiers and snowboarders find out on the slopes.

3 TECHNOLOGY AND ATHLETIC PERFORMANCE

There is more to performance than just training hard and being physically fit. It is for this reason that scientists, coaches, and athletes themselves search for ways to use technology to improve performance.

The importance of technique

When it comes to excelling at sports, technique is just as important as physical fitness. Technique is how you perform a movement or set of movements. In most sports, there is a correct way of doing things. For example, the correct technique to throw a football is as follows:

- Grip the ball with your ring finger (next to your little finger) and little fingers crossing the laces, and your thumb underneath.
- Get into a throwing stance. To do this, position your feet no more than shoulder width apart and lean your weight on your back leg.
- Pull the ball up to your shoulder, level with your ear.
- Turn your body into the throw, releasing the ball with the fingertips as your throwing arm moves forward.

≫ There is a correct way to throw a football. Good technique is important and needs to be taught and practiced. It is more efficient and can also prevent injury.

ARISTOTLE

Although the science of biomechanics is a relatively modern thing, its origins can be traced back to ancient Greece. Philosopher Aristotle (384–322 BCE) was fascinated by the way animals and humans moved, and he studied the way muscles, joints, and bones worked. He contributed to the first book on the subject, *De Motu Animalium* ("On the Movement of Animals"), and is now considered by some academics to be "the father of biomechanics."

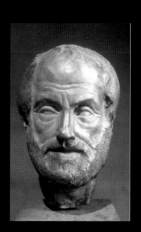

Using good technique means you can perform the action—whether kicking a soccer ball, running, or dribbling a basketball—efficiently. If you perform a set of movements efficiently, you will use less energy. Using less energy means you won't tire as quickly as the race, game, or match wears on.

Biomechanics for beginners

The study of human movement is called **biomechanics**. Coaches who specialize in biomechanics are able to watch athletes performing and explain to them where they are making mistakes. They can also suggest ways in which athletes can improve their technique in order to save energy, perform the movement more efficiently, and therefore have the best chance of improving their performance.

CASE STUDY / MOTION ANALYSIS

Professional athletes often ask to receive motion analysis. This is a high-tech method of studying the movement of joints and muscles in the body using high-speed cameras. The athlete is filmed from a number of angles. Biomechanics coaches can then replay the video footage in slow motion and point out even the tiniest flaws in their technique.

Three-dimensional analysis

The most cutting-edge biomechanical analysis currently available is based around a technology famously used in movies. Motion-capture technology has been used in countless movies, from *The Hobbit* to the *Planet of the Apes* series, to give animated characters more lifelike movements.

THE SCIENCE BEHIND: MOTION-CAPTURE TECHNOLOGY

Bike fitting is a process that uses motion-capture technology to set up a bike to fit the exact biomechanics of each rider.

⌃ Motion-capture technology isn't just used for cyclists, or even just athletes. This is an actor in a motion-capture suit "filming" a scene for a television show.

• Before the motion-capture process can begin, special reflective markers that look like flat white discs are attached to the cyclist's body.

• As the cyclist pedals, high-resolution cameras film his or her movements. These cameras are connected to a computer running 3-D motion-capture software, which is able to identify the position of the reflective markers relative to the cameras.

• The software uses this to create a moving 3-D computer image of the cyclist as he or she pedals.

• These images are then used to figure out the best riding position. This is usually the position that allows the cyclist to pedal most efficiently.

The same technology is also behind video game systems that respond to human movement, such as the Nintendo Wii and X-Box Kinect. Motion-capture technology was actually developed by biomechanical engineers to help study human movement back in the 1990s. This kind of analysis creates three-dimensional computer images of the body during exercise.

⌃ There is now sports diagnostic technology to measure people swimming in the water. Here, technology is monitoring a triathlete's performance.

Swimming against the tide

You might think that performing biomechanical analysis on a swimmer would be virtually impossible. How would you monitor people in the water, while creating different conditions for people to swim in? Filming swimmers from different angles as they power up and down a pool is very difficult.

Thankfully, scientists have found a solution. It involves a special machine called the "endless pool" or "counter-**current** swimming machine."

CASE STUDY / THE ENDLESS POOL

The endless pool is a very small swimming pool, or sometimes a glass or Perspex tank, in which an athlete swims against an artificially created current. It works like an aquatic version of a running treadmill. No matter how much the swimmer struggles against the current, he or she stays in the same position. Just like a treadmill, the speed and resistance of the water can be adjusted to suit the swimmer's strengths and weaknesses.

While the athlete swims, his or her coach can film the swimmer from different angles using a number of cameras. Together, they will later watch the footage and use it to suggest improvements to the swimmer's technique.

Running faster using computers

The 100-meter sprint is the most glamorous and famous of all track-and-field athletics events. As the shortest and fastest event, races are often decided by a desperate lunge for the line, with runners finishing just centimeters apart. With such fine margins deciding the outcome, it is perhaps unsurprising that scientists are interested in looking for ways to use technology to improve performance.

CASE STUDY / ANALYZING SPRINTERS

In 2011, researchers at the University of Maine decided to take a high-tech approach to analyzing sprint performances. First, they used motion-capture technology to study runners' biomechanics, to see how they ran. This technology was discussed on page 13. At the same time, they inserted pads in the sprinters' running shoes. The pads respond to pressure and helped to calculate the force and power generated during race starts. After studying the information, coach David Cusano suggested changes to both technique and training programs.

After following their new programs, most athletes recorded new personal-best times. One sprinter even knocked two seconds off her 400-meter best. In an event that takes top athletes between 44 and 50 seconds to complete, that is a significant amount of time.

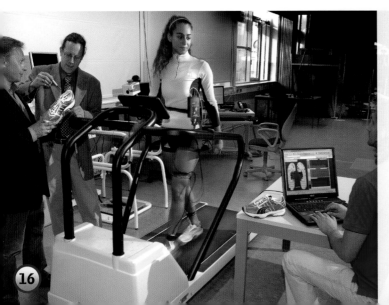

≪ Here, the movements and fitness of an athlete are being monitored at the Laboratory for Movement Science and Sport Technology in Germany.

Laser-guided analysis

The FAST system (short for Force, Acceleration, Sprint, Time) came into use in 2012.

Unique to this technology are special **starting blocks**. They detect the tiniest muscle twitch and are used to measure a number of **variables**. These include how quickly the sprinter reacts to the starting gun and the force applied by each foot to the blocks.

Once the sprinter has left the blocks, they're followed down the track by a laser beam directed at their back. This laser tracks the position of the athlete throughout the sprint, and sends 400 positioning measurements a second to the analyst's laptop computer.

TECHNOLOGY THROUGH TIME: ON YOUR MARKS!

The current record time for the men's 100-meter sprint is 9.58 seconds. It is held by Jamaican superstar Usain Bolt. That time is over a second quicker than the first record set in 1912 by Dom Lippincott.

There are many reasons for this. In the early days, nobody used starting blocks, which help sprinters get the best start possible. Second, we now understand more than ever before about the science behind sprinting. Today's sprinters can tweak their technique to get the most power and speed throughout their races.

⌃ This is Usain Bolt. Pressure pads inside starting blocks help him and other sprinters analyze their reactions to the starting gun.

Knowledge is power

Today, coaches know more about how their players perform than ever before. By using high-tech computer software, coaches can now track the movements and physical performance of any team player over the course of a game or even a season.

This wasn't always the case. In the past, coaches only had a limited amount of facts and figures, such as the number of baskets made, goals scored, or bases stolen. More often than not, coaches had to judge player performances simply on what they saw with their own eyes.

Performance data

Today, sports coaches have mountains of information at their fingertips, covering every aspect of their players' performances. This information is known, in sports circles, as performance data. Its use has revolutionized sports coaching over the last 20 years.

The use of performance data systems can help different kinds of sports coaches in many ways. In addition to understanding the strengths and weaknesses of their own players, coaches can now study the performance data of opposing teams to figure out how to beat them. One way to do this is by using the FIELDf/x system.

CASE STUDY / BALL TRACKING SYSTEMS

In 2011, the Boston Red Sox became the first professional baseball team to use the FIELDf/x system, which tracks the actions of every player on the field during a game. To do this, the system uses cameras positioned around the stadium, as well as special performance analysis computer software. After the game, coaches can look at where every ball was hit, where the fielders were positioned, and how many successful catches were made. They can even compare the performances of team members to those of players on opposing teams.

Many baseball teams now use FIELDf/x, while similar cutting-edge systems are also used in other sports. For example, the ProZone system, which was first introduced in the 1990s, has revolutionized soccer.

Like FIELDf/x, ProZone uses television cameras to track players' movement—and the ball—around the field. It goes further than FIELDf/x, though, by including information on the players' physical performances. Players are asked to wear **GPS** tracking devices and heart-rate monitors, which monitor their energy levels and effort as well as their actions.

⋁ Thanks to new performance data systems, baseball coaches now understand more than ever before about how their players perform during games.

4 TECHNOLOGY AND SPORTS NUTRITION

In the past, athletes did not understand the effect that different types of food and drink had. Today, even many **amateur** athletes have a basic understanding of **sports nutrition** and its effect on performance.

In recent decades, scientists have found ways to maximize the impact of diet on sports performance. These include the creation of new "super foods" in laboratories and the development of high-tech computer programs to tailor diets to an individual athlete's needs.

Nutrition basics

Food is full of stored energy that our body can use in many ways. The energy in a particular food or drink, measured in calories, is listed on the packaging. Packaging also lists the exact amounts of different types of energy in the food, such as carbohydrates, fats, sugars, vitamins, and protein.

- Carbohydrates are the body's equivalent of gasoline. They keep the body going. Carbohydrates contain sugars that the body removes and stores in blood cells for use throughout the day.
- Protein contains amino acids that the body uses to grow and maintain healthy cells. Protein also helps repair tired and damaged muscles after exercise, which is why many athletes have protein-heavy "recovery drinks" right after training.
- Fat is used to store energy and protect our internal organs. Our bodies need a certain amount of fat, but too much in our diet is bad for us. Fat is harder to "burn off" during exercise than the energy we get from carbohydrates.
- Vitamins are found naturally in all kinds of foods. You need certain, small amounts for growth and good health in the body.

A balanced meal

Sports **nutritionists** understand the ways in which different foods give us energy, and how athletes' bodies use that energy. This means they can create diets that match each athlete's individual needs.

NUTRITIONAL NEEDS

Comparing the daily energy needs of teenagers and professional athletes

GIRLS

Carbohydrate	at least 130 grams, but possibly more, depending on weight and activity level
Protein	46 grams

BOYS

Carbohydrate	at least 130 grams, but possibly more (see above)
Protein	52 grams

LONG-DISTANCE CYCLIST

Number of calories needed: 5,000–8,000 per day, during a race. **What they should eat**: Lots and lots of carbohydrates—around 850 grams per day—plus 0.6 grams of protein for every pound of body weight (roughly 85 grams for a 170-pound/ 85-kilogram rider).

WEIGHTLIFTER

Number of calories needed: 3,000–4,000 a day, when training and performing. **What they should eat**: Lots of protein to help build and repair muscles. A 176-pound (80-kilogram) Olympic weightlifter would consume around 160 grams of protein per day.

SWIMMER

Number of calories needed: 2,800–4,000 per day, depending on body size of the swimmer and his or her training volume. **What they should eat**: Lots of carbohydrates, such as pasta, and some protein to help with muscle repair.

Keeping track of nutrients

Many professional athletes struggle to figure out the exact amounts of carbohydrates, protein, fats, vitamins, and minerals in their food, so they use sports nutritionists. These are experts who understand what athletes in different sports need to eat in order to train and perform at their very best. Some sports teams also employ chefs to prepare healthy, nutritious meals for their athletes.

Nutrition and computers

Most sports nutritionists now use special computer software programs to create nutrition plans for athletes and keep track of their progress.

CASE STUDY / NUTRITION SOFTWARE

Nutrition computer programs are built around enormous databases of ingredients and their nutritional values. First, a nutritionist will input the ingredients for a meal into the software. The program then automatically figures out the number of calories and essential types of energy in that meal.

One of the most popular programs is called Genesis R&D. It features the nutritional details of 55,000 different ingredients, plus over 150 nutrients and food groups. Users simply make a list of ingredients and their quantities, and the software does the rest.

Another popular sports nutrition program is Food Processor SQL. While it works in a similar way to Genesis R&D, it also comes with an app (short for "application") called FoodProdigy. This allows athletes and nutritionists to plan and track their food intake, wherever they are in the world.

Each athlete is given a personal profile, including age, weight, height, gender, and a list of all planned exercise activities. From this, the software can calculate whether they are getting the right amount of carbohydrates, protein, and so on. The program contains a database of 654 different activities, with details of energy usage, and a list of 35,000 ingredients.

TECHNOLOGY THROUGH TIME: RUNNING ON EMPTY

While sports nutrition is now a long-established science, this wasn't always the case. In 1904, very little was understood about how food and drinks affected the body. In fact, some contestants in the 1904 Olympics marathon were given eggs and brandy to keep them going during the race. One of the key features of brandy is the drug alcohol. Alcohol makes you dehydrate faster and lose some of your coordination. Scientific research on nutrition and exercise began in the 1930s, but it wasn't until the 1970s that it really began to take off. Up until that point, most athletes took a "trial and error" approach to nutrition, and some didn't even think about their diet at all. Today, sports nutrition researchers, exercise scientists, and even chefs often work together, developing training plans and nutrition plans at the same time.

∨ Researchers and scientists help chefs to prepare meals for professional athletes that contain just the right amount of carbohydrates, protein, vitamins, and minerals.

Supplementing athletes' diets

Sports nutrition doesn't end with carefully planned meals and a high numbers of calories. Scientists' understanding of nutrition and what makes the body tick has led to a rise in the number of specially created **supplements**. These are tablets, powders, bars, gels, and drinks that supposedly help build muscle growth or replace minerals and vitamins lost during exercise. Some of them can even give you a much-needed energy boost.

Proving the benefits of supplements

Developing supplements is a long and complicated process. Many are created in high-tech laboratories, using the latest cutting-edge scientific equipment.

Once supplements have been created, they must be thoroughly tested to make sure that they do what their creators claim they are supposed to do. This involves volunteers taking the supplements before, during, or after exercise, while scientists monitor the way their bodies respond.

Scientists from the World Anti-Doping Agency also test new sports supplements. This is to make sure that they don't contain traces of any banned substances. These are drugs or **stimulants** that have been banned because they give athletes an unfair advantage over their rivals.

PIONEERS

DR. ROBERT CADE

In 1965, Dr. Robert Cade was a professor at the University of Florida Medical School, studying the effects of exercise on the human body. He discovered that players on the university's football team, the Gators, didn't just lose water when they sweated, but also essential sugars, salts, and minerals. As a result, he went away and designed a drink for the players that would quickly replace these lost nutrients. He called it Gatorade, and it became the world's first "sports drink."

Boosting performance

There is currently a huge range of supplements available to athletes. Some of these, such as creatine, are already in the body in small amounts. Creatine is a chemical produced in the liver that the body uses to boost energy. The supplement version is available as a powder that can be mixed into drinks. It includes much higher levels of creatine than the body would naturally produce and therefore allows athletes using this to train harder.

Other supplements come about by accident. One of the most talked about supplements of 2014 was Generation UCAN, a sports drink based around a new type of "super-starch" carbohydrate developed in a laboratory. It releases energy to the body over a longer period of time, compared with other, ordinary carbohydrates. Therefore, it helps athletes to exercise for longer periods without needing to take on extra energy. Amazingly, the super-starch behind the supplement was discovered when scientists were looking for a cure for a rare disease.

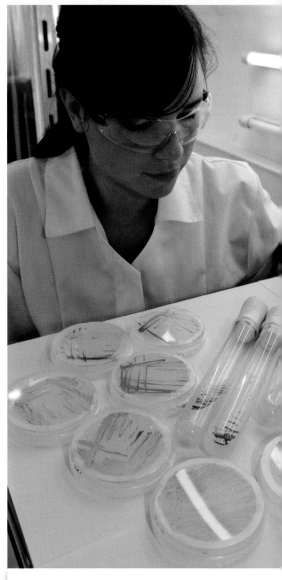

⌃ Sport scientists use the latest cutting-edge equipment and testing techniques to develop nutrition supplements that boost athletes' performances.

Breaking the rules

Some athletes are not satisfied with taking regular, legal sports supplements. Their desire to win is so great that they are willing to cheat to succeed. These athletes take illegal and often dangerous substances to improve their performance. This process is commonly known as "doping," and the athletes who do it are taking these risky, performance-enhancing drugs.

The use of performance-enhancing drugs is a huge issue in sports. Almost every major sport you can think of, from the 100-meter sprint to baseball, has at some point had to deal with athletes breaking the rules this way. It is such a big problem that professional athletes have to undergo drug testing on a regular basis. If caught, athletes can be banned from competing for months or years.

CASE STUDY / LANCE ARMSTRONG

Lance Armstrong was once thought of as one of the most inspirational men in sports. He'd survived cancer and won the world's most grueling cycling race, the Tour de France, a record seven times. People thought he was superhuman. Sadly for his fans, he'd been cheating. In 2013, he finally admitted that he'd taken performance-enhancing drugs to win races. Throughout his career, Armstrong took Erythropoietin, a drug commonly known as EPO. It boosts the production of red blood cells, allowing athletes to exercise harder for longer. Armstrong also admitted to getting **blood transfusions** during races, which had a similar effect on his performance. He was stripped of his race wins and told to repay the millions of dollars he had won during his career.

Cheating the tests

Even the threat of being caught and banned doesn't stop some athletes from breaking the rules. As soon as drug testers develop a new test for a banned substance, chemists try to develop a new drug that the testers can't detect. This is what happened with a drug called THG (short for "Tetrahydrogestrinone"), which was nicknamed "the clear" by its creator, American chemist Patrick Arnold.

THE SCIENCE BEHIND: THG: "THE CLEAR"

THG was an anabolic steroid that increased muscle strength and made recovery after exercise quicker. This meant that athletes who used it could train harder, more often. THG was created in a laboratory, and at first, drug tests couldn't detect it. This made it very tempting to cheaters, who saw it as a fast track to race wins, gold medals, and world records.

Then, a frustrated coach, annoyed that cheaters were beating his "clean" athletes, sent a sample of the drug to the anti-doping authorities. Within a few months, a number of high-profile American athletes, including sprinter Tim Montgomery and baseball star Barry Bonds, were banned for using "the clear." It was one of the biggest doping scandals world sports had seen.

⌄ American sprinter Marion Jones was stripped of her gold medal from the 2000 Sydney Olympics after admitting that she'd taken an illegal performance-enhancing drug called THG.

5

TECHNOLOGY AND SPORTS EQUIPMENT

Given that all sports require some kind of equipment, it is not surprising that much effort has gone into developing "gear" that improves performance. Some technological changes have had a huge effect on the way a sport is played:

⌃ The development of stiff but flexible human-made materials has helped pole vaulters to set new world records.

- Football got faster following the development of artificial grass (also known as Astroturf) in the 1960s.
- Fiberglass and **carbon-fiber composite** poles have allowed pole vaulters to jump higher. When vaulters used bamboo, wood, and metal poles, the men's world record was 15.65 feet (4.77 meters). With carbon-fiber poles, this is now an amazing 20.21 feet (6.16 meters)!

Safety first

Other technological advancements make sports safer for participants. Following the tragic death of seven-time NASCAR Sprint Cup champion Dale Earnhardt during a race in 2001, efforts have been made to improve driver safety.

Dale Earnhardt would not have died if he had been wearing the HANS device that all drivers must now use. This protects the neck during crashes. NASCAR drivers must also now wear a high-tech seatbelt called a six-point harness, which straps them in tightly but allows for a quick exit from the car.

Small changes, big results

The theory of "marginal gains" is the idea that lots of small changes in equipment, clothing, and training techniques can lead to better results. The idea became popular following the success of the British track cycling team at the 2008 and 2012 Olympic Games.

CASE STUDY / BRITISH CYCLING

The man behind the theory of "marginal gains" is a cycling coach named Dave Brailsford. He started working with British Cycling in 1998, with the aim of turning Great Britain into the most successful track cycling nation in the world.

Brailsford employed a team of coaches and researchers to examine every single aspect of training, performance, and equipment. This led to a number of small technological advancements that added up to big results.

- Bike tires were sprayed with alcohol before races to make them "stickier" (helping riders to make more powerful starts).

- Tiny, matchbox-sized "black boxes" were placed under riders' seats to collect performance data.

- Clothing manufacturer Speedo made "skinsuits" for swimming (see page 32 for more).

- Life-size models of riders were created and used in wind tunnel tests, so that scientists could figure out the most efficient riding position.

Everything that could be examined was, and the results were amazing. At Beijing 2008, British track cyclists won 12 medals. Four years later in London, the team won nine more medals, seven of which were gold.

Movement through the air

One of the biggest areas of technological advancement in recent years has come in the science of aerodynamics. This is the study of how air moves around objects.

Aerodynamics has a huge impact on many sports, from Formula 1 motor racing to golf. Even racing wheelchairs, used by para-athletes in the Paralympics and other international competitions, are designed with aerodynamics in mind.

Aerodynamics plays a part in any sport that involves a ball, clothing, or equipment that travels at speed. It is for this reason that much sports equipment goes through aerodynamic testing during development. If something is more aerodynamic, chances are that it will help an athlete's or team's performance. It might not be by much, but as we have already seen, "marginal gains" can make a huge difference.

CASE STUDY / THE 2014 FIFA WORLD CUP BALL

When developing its Brazuca ball for soccer's 2014 FIFA World Cup in Brazil, Adidas spent a lot of time and money on aerodynamic testing. Players had complained about the unpredictable movement through the air of some of its previous World Cup balls.

The final Brazuca ball featured fewer leather panels than previous balls and special stitching that reduced the amount of turbulence in the air when the ball was kicked. As a result, the Brazuca ball made it easier for players to accurately pass and shoot during matches.

THE SCIENCE BEHIND: AERODYNAMICS

The flow of air around a ball in flight can be studied using streams of smoke in a wind tunnel.

Experiments in a wind tunnel have shown that there is a pocket of unstable, turbulent low-pressure air behind the ball (known as a wake), and because the ball must push against a front of higher pressure, the resulting pressure difference causes what is known as "drag."

Scientists have shown that when the surface of a ball is not smooth, the size of the low pressure wake behind the ball is smaller. This means that the pressure difference is reduced, and so is the "drag."

A good example of this in action is the golf ball; the dimpled surface of the golf ball enables the ball to travel farther than a golf ball with a smooth surface.

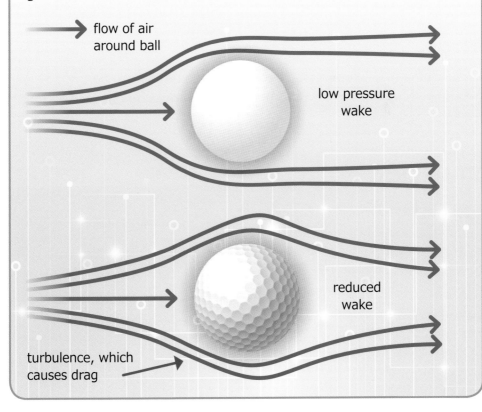

flow of air around ball

low pressure wake

reduced wake

turbulence, which causes drag

Overcoming natural forces

Some sports, such as the popular Winter Olympics events bobsled, skeleton, and luge, have to battle with more natural forces than aerodynamics. As sliders hurtle down the ice-covered bobsled run at speeds of up to 90 miles (145 kilometers) an hour, they also experience these other forces:

- **friction** (created by the connection between the sliders' sleds and the ice below)
- the force of gravity (known as g-force).

≫ The U.S. Olympic bobsled team worked with engineers from carmakers BMW to create a high-tech sled for the 2014 Sochi Winter Olympics.

Finding effective solutions to overcome these issues can be the difference between taking the gold home and missing out on a medal completely.

PIONEERS

FIONA FAIRHURST

It was sports clothing designer Fiona Fairhurst's interest in sharks that gave her the idea to create the groundbreaking "Fastskin" swimsuit. She noticed that the surface of a shark's skin features bumps and grooves. These help control the flow of water around the shark's body and reduce drag (see page 31). She took her idea to the swimwear company Speedo, which helped her develop a swimsuit. In 2004, her revolutionary swimsuit helped 47 swimmers win medals at the Athens Olympics.

Cutting-edge design

It is perhaps unsurprising, then, that millions of dollars are spent every year on designing, testing, and manufacturing high-tech sleds. Ahead of the 2014 Winter Olympics in Sochi, Russia, a number of teams joined forces with carmakers and Formula 1 racing teams to design sleds they believed would give them an edge over competitors.

Team USA worked with BMW, Team GB (Great Britain and Northern Ireland) worked with the McLaren F1 team, and Germany worked with Ferrari. They didn't just look at the shape and design of their sleds, but also the materials they were built out of. In a sport where hundredths of a second make a difference, you have to try everything.

Moving faster through water

Swimmers also had that same desire to gain a competitive advantage, causing a long-running **controversy** in the sport. Sports organizations have banned some skin-type suits because they think they gave competitors an unfair advantage.

THE SCIENCE BEHIND: HYDRODYNAMICS

For years, swimwear manufacturers have been obsessed with hydrodynamics, which is the study of the way water moves around an object. Water acts a little like air, in that the water against the swimmer's body is like the drag on the rough surface of a ball. Swimwear manufacturers soon realized that by putting swimmers in smooth, skintight bodysuits, they could help them move through the water quicker. During the 2000 Sydney Olympics, swimmers in full-body "skinsuits" dominated races, beating rivals in ordinary swimwear by wide margins. Over the next eight years, swimmers wearing these "fast suits" broke almost all swimming world records.

Materials that make a difference

The swimming skinsuits that caused such controversy were made of a range of high-tech fabrics, which were specially designed in laboratories to improve performance. The makers of these fabrics claim their materials reduce drag, as the suits' fabric helps to keep swimmers' muscles warm and trap air. This makes swimmers feel like they are racing over the water, rather than through it.

This all shows that materials can make a difference. In fact, what people use to make sports equipment can have just as big an effect on performance as the design itself. This is particularly true in the case of the material carbon fiber.

CASE STUDY / CARBON FIBER

A carbon-fiber composite contains long, thin strands of a material called graphite; these fibers are bound together in a polymer matrix. The fibers are often woven into fabric; sometimes 3-D weaves are created, which gives increased strength. The key properties of a composite like this are high stiffness and strength, but also low weight.

A good example of this in action is to think about two bicycle frames, one made from carbon-fiber composite and one made from steel. The composite frame would weigh far less, but it would be as stiff as the steel frame. The result? The athlete will not need to work as hard to maintain the same speed.

British cyclist Chris Boardman proved this when he won a gold medal at the 1992 Olympics. His revolutionary Lotus 108 bike featured a lightweight frame made almost entirely out of carbon-fiber composites.

« Chris Boardman won an Olympic gold medal for the 4,000-meter Individual Pursuit competition at the 1992 Olympics in Barcelona.

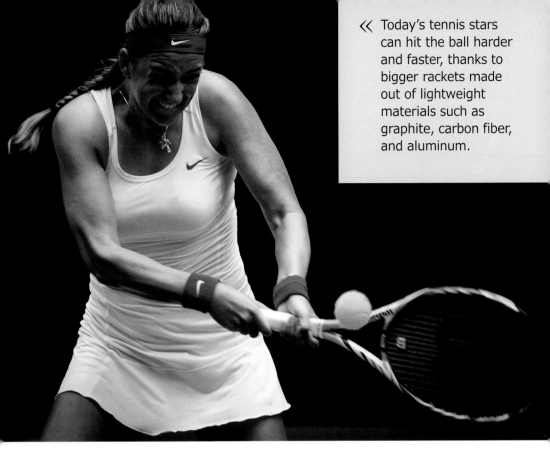

<< Today's tennis stars can hit the ball harder and faster, thanks to bigger rackets made out of lightweight materials such as graphite, carbon fiber, and aluminum.

Revolutionary rackets and bats

Up until the mid-1970s, most tennis rackets were made of wood, and the area of the rackets used to hit the ball was quite small. Then, professional players started using bigger rackets made out of lightweight metals such as aluminum. Composite materials were soon introduced, making rackets even lighter.

In general, this approach to exploring other materials meant the nature of the game changed forever. Lightweight rackets, coupled with a bigger surface with which to hit the ball, led to faster serves. This, in turn, led to a serve-dominated game.

Aluminum bats had a similar effect on baseball. Because aluminum bats were sometimes less dense and lighter than wooden ones, this made them easier to bat with. That meant players could hit balls harder, faster, and farther. This led to concerns for player safety. Now, aluminum bats are banned in Major League Baseball.

The Paralympics revolution

The use of lightweight materials and high-tech equipment design has had a particularly big impact on sports for people with disabilities. Although athletes with disabilities have been competing internationally in selected sports since 1952, it took until the 1980s for the Paralympics to become an established offshoot of the Olympics. By then, attitudes toward disabilities were starting to change, and technology had allowed for stronger competition over a greater range of sports.

Today, the Paralympics are a huge global event, with thousands of athletes competing across a wide range of sports. Many of these events are versions of long-established able-bodied events. The 2012 Paralympics saw record crowds cheer on the athletes, many of whom put in unforgettable performances.

⋁ The use of aerodynamic testing and lightweight materials such as carbon fiber has dramatically changed the nature and style of wheelchair racing.

TECHNOLOGY THROUGH TIME: RACING WHEELCHAIRS

In the early days of sports for disabled people, racers used traditional two-wheeled chairs, weighing between 16 and 40 pounds (7 and 18 kilograms). In comparison, today's custom-made racing wheelchairs weigh between 9 and 22 pounds (4 and 10 kilograms). They are made out of carbon-fiber composites, have an innovative, streamlined three-wheel design, and are usually put through rigorous aerodynamic testing. As a result, wheelchair races are now much quicker than they were 20 years ago.

THE SCIENCE BEHIND: RUNNING BLADES

It's not only wheelchair-bound athletes whose competitiveness has been transformed by technology. Once upon a time, it was difficult for athletes with prosthetic limbs, particularly those with artificial legs, to compete in sports. The development of special "running blades" in the 1980s changed that.

Each running blade is made from around 80 layers of carbon fiber. Blades are tailored to fit the individual running style and disability of each athlete, so no two blades are ever the same. However, they all work according to the same principle.

Carbon-fiber running blades allow athletes without lower leg function to power around the track just like able-bodied runners.

- Each blade features a composite structure that operates like a spring that propels the runner forward.

- When the bottom, or "forefoot," of the blade touches the ground, it compresses like a spring. Just like a spring, the blade stores energy.

- The blade then rebounds, pushing the stored energy back toward the runner's legs. Ninety percent of the energy generated by the runner's stride is returned, helping to propel him or her down the track at an impressive speed.

6

TECHNOLOGY AND SPORTS MEDICINE

For professional athletes, being able to train and perform is incredibly important. It is their job, after all, and one that they really enjoy. So, injured athletes want to be back on their feet as quickly as possible. Thankfully, advances in sports medicine are helping them to do just that.

Taking care of muscles

Athletes push their bodies to the limit, so it is inevitable that they will develop injuries every now and then. Their muscles, which work hardest during exercise, are usually the first to be injured. That is why sports doctors and inventors have spent a lot of time developing new treatments and technologies that help muscles recover after exercise.

The artificial physiotherapist

Athletes used to keep themselves in shape through regular appointments with a **physiotherapist**. This is a health professional who specializes in human movement. Physiotherapists are trained to massage muscles before and after exercise, suggest gentle exercises to keep the body flexible, and design injury recovery programs.

CASE STUDY / PNEUMATIC RECOVERY UNIT

One of the most popular sports medicine inventions of recent times was designed to mimic the feel of being massaged by a physiotherapist. The pneumatic recovery unit is a large, leg-length boot or sleeve. The athlete sits or lies down while wearing the unit, and air is pumped in around the legs.

According to the makers, this stimulates the muscles and gets blood pumping around them quicker. This triggers the body's natural repair process, leading to quicker recovery times. The pneumatic recovery unit is very popular with NBA stars. Indiana Pacers player Roy Hibbert even uses one at home, to keep his legs feeling "fresh" between matches.

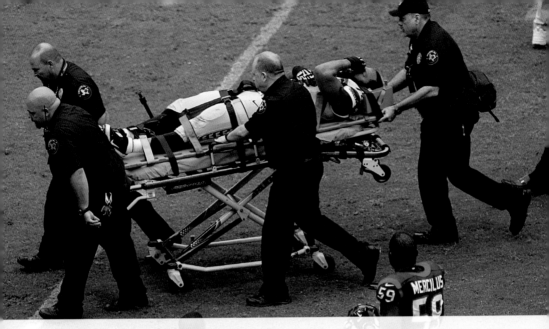

∧ Modern sports medicine helped football player Michael Bennett get back to action just a week after being taken from the field on a stretcher during a game.

Laser therapy

Another new treatment technique popular with NBA players is low-level light therapy. Although the science behind the treatment has yet to be proven, some players say their muscles feel better after having it. The therapy involves firing a laser beam at key "trigger points" in muscles for a short period of time. The lasers supposedly stimulate cells inside the muscles, making the body replace damaged tissue at a quicker rate.

PIONEERS

THE ASSOCIATION INTERNATIONAL MEDICO-SPORTIVE

At the 1920 Winter Olympics in St. Moritz, Switzerland, a group of doctors from around the world held a meeting. They would go on to form the Association International Medico-Sportive (AIMS). This was the first organization dedicated to the treatment and welfare of athletes. The organization is still around today, though it is now known as the International Federation of Sports Medicine.

Surgeons to the rescue

Despite all the technological advances in sports medicine, some of the most common injuries in sports can only be treated by surgery. That used to mean a stay in a hospital, a long operation, and sometimes months or years of recovery.

Things are a little different now. Modern methods of surgery allow athletes to be back in training within weeks of their injuries taking place.

⌄ Modern keyhole surgery has helped to dramatically reduce recovery times for many common sports injuries, such as ligament damage.

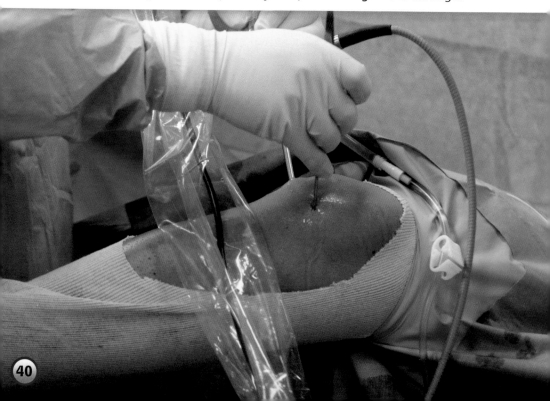

At one point or another, most athletes who take part in sports that involve running will damage their knees. The most common knee injuries involve the ligaments that hold the joint together. Ligaments are a type of tough, flexible tissue that acts a bit like rubber bands. Through the strain of frequent exercise, ligaments can tear, leading to swelling, pain, and an inability to run or move freely.

Repairing damaged knee ligaments used to be quite difficult, and even the most skilled surgeons couldn't guarantee that athletes would be back competing anytime soon. Today, surgeons use a technique called keyhole surgery to quickly repair damaged ligaments.

Keyhole surgery is incredibly precise. Surgeons make a small incision (cut) close to the affected area and use tiny, microscopic cameras to get a clear view of the damaged ligaments. Using similarly small instruments, the surgeons are able to repair the ligaments by taking tissue from another part of the knee and attaching it to the damaged area.

Although the procedure is usually done by hand, it is now also possible in some instances to perform the surgery using robotic equipment. In these cases, the surgeon controls the robotic instruments using a computer.

Better recovery times

Keyhole knee surgery has helped many leading athletes recover from career-threatening injuries, including basketball player Al Jefferson and soccer player Luis Suarez.

Football star Robert Griffin III has had keyhole surgery on his knees on two separate occasions. The second time, in January 2013, surgeons repaired two different ligaments. In the past, this level of surgery could have seen him sidelined for at least a year. As it turned out, the Washington Redskins' quarterback returned to action in September 2013, just eight months after leaving the field with a career-threatening injury.

⌃ Correct stretching techniques help to prevent injuries. You should stretch properly before and after exercise.

Injury prevention

It might seem obvious, but the easiest way for athletes to stay fit and healthy is to prevent injuries altogether. Given that injuries to key players can cost sports teams both on and off the field, it is perhaps unsurprising that injury prevention is now taken very seriously.

Professional athletes used to try to prevent injuries by getting regular massages from a physiotherapist. They might also see a doctor every few weeks or undergo regular fitness testing to determine their overall levels of fitness.

High-tech approaches

While these methods are still popular, many athletes and sports teams are now turning to more high-tech techniques to help them prevent injuries. In 2013, an Irish software firm launched an application called Injury Profiler. This uses huge amounts of performance data, taken from fitness tests, training sessions, and game appearances, to figure out the likelihood of an athlete getting injured. The system can then suggest the best injury prevention techniques and even changes to athletes' training programs.

A growing number of athletes and sports teams are also turning to biomechanical analysis and motion analysis to help prevent injuries. In addition to being used to improve technique (see pages 12–13), this kind of treatment can identify potential weaknesses in the way an athlete runs, jumps, or throws. If the weaknesses go unchecked, they can lead to unwanted injuries.

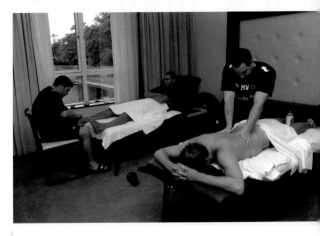

⌃ Regular massage and physiotherapy are still important to professional athletes, along with the new, high-tech methods of injury prevention.

CASE STUDY / CHECK

If you knew the exact moment when your body was ready for exercise, it would be less likely that you'd get injured during training. That is the idea behind CHECK, a pioneering electronic system that claims to help prevent injuries.

CHECK comes in three parts: wires that connect to your thumb and forearm, a small handheld device, and an application for smartphones and tablet computers. Each morning, athletes using the system go through the following steps:

1. Attach the wires, coming from the device, to their body and place the device in the palm of their hand.

2. Switch on the device. This sends a small burst of electricity down the wires. This stimulates the muscles in the body.

3. The way athletes' muscles respond to this electricity is logged by the device, which feeds the information to the smartphone application.

4. The application then analyzes the data and assesses athletes' readiness for training. If their muscles are in good shape, they get an "all clear." If not, they are advised to take it easy or train later in the day.

7 TECHNOLOGY AND SPORTS IN THE MEDIA

Sports are a big business, with the results of games and matches often hinging on referees or **umpires** making the correct decisions. More and more often, people in sports are turning to technology to make sure their officials make the right judgment calls.

Instant replay

The most widely used technology is the television replay. Multiple camera angles, slow-motion footage, and high-definition displays make TV footage perfect for decision-making. Many major team sports now use television officials. These are umpires or referees who can be called on to help with difficult decisions by watching television replays.

Many sports use this technology to help officials make decisions.
- In football, officials and coaches can request instant replays of close calls.
- TV replay is used in cricket (a sport somewhat similar to baseball) to determine whether a player's foot has gone over the line when it is not allowed to do so.

Amazing accuracy

Some sports have gone further, introducing high-tech systems to help officials to make the correct decision. The most common of these is ball-tracking technology, a system that can predict—to within millimeters, in some cases—the movement of a ball.

Ball-tracking technology has been used in a number of "ball sports" following its invention in 2001. After being used in tennis, it was introduced into soccer in time for the 2014 FIFA World Cup in Brazil.

THE SCIENCE BEHIND: BALL-TRACKING TECHNOLOGY

Ball-tracking systems such as HawkEye and GoalControl, as used at the 2014 FIFA World Cup, combine multiple television cameras with special computer software to predict the flight of a ball between two or more points. High-speed cameras placed around the field are used to keep track of the ball. In tennis, the ball is tracked from the point a player hits it, until it strikes the ground on the other side of the court.

These images are quickly fed into a computer, which creates a virtual 3-D reconstruction of what just happened. This event reconstruction shows the flight of the ball and predicts with 99.9 percent accuracy what would have happened next. Where this technology is used, tennis umpires use this information to see whether a ball was in play or not when it hit the ground. In soccer, it is used to tell referees if a disputed goal should be awarded. When the ball crosses the goal line, a message is sent to the referee's watch. This makes the watch vibrate, telling the referee to award a goal.

⌃ Ball-tracking technology has revolutionized the way officials make decisions in a number of sports, including tennis and soccer.

Television innovations

Ball-tracking systems started life as toys used by television broadcasters to improve their coverage. TV companies are constantly coming up with high-tech ways to enhance viewers' enjoyment of sports.

Many of these inventions have become part of the decision-making process. There are others that still might become important to sports officials. Some examples are:

- small cameras mounted onto the hats and helmets worn by players and officials in football
- live broadcasts of team radio communications in motorsports, such as Formula 1
- "Hot Spot," which uses thermal imaging cameras, first developed for use by the military in war zones, to detect friction between ball and bat. As the ball and bat come into contact, energy is created in the form of heat. On television coverage of baseball, "Hot Spot" shows where a batter hit the ball, or whether he or she even hit it at all. On the television pictures, a bright white mark will appear at the point at which the bat and ball made contact.

Electronic scoring and timekeeping

Today, many sports rely on electronics to keep track of point scoring, timekeeping, and whether or not competitors are breaking the rules. Electronic timekeeping systems can be found in many professional sports. Great examples include:

- pressure-sensitive starting blocks used at track athletics competitions. These are used to make sure that nobody gains an unfair advantage by starting too early. If an athlete applies pressure to the blocks within one-tenth of a second of the starting gun being fired, a false start is called. This means the athlete may then be disqualified from the race.
- touchpads attached to the ends of lanes during swimming races. At the end of each length, swimmers touch the pad at the end of their lane. The touchpad then sends a signal to a computer, which records and displays their time.

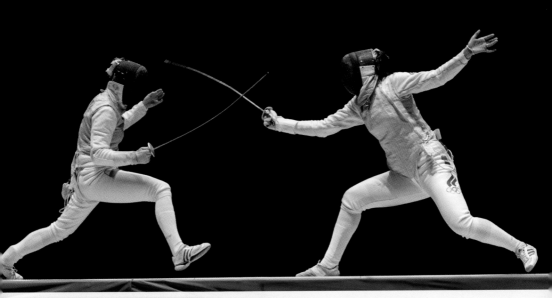

CASE STUDY / FENCING SCOREKEEPING

The Olympic sport of fencing is a fast-moving sport in which competitors try to score points in very carefully timed attacks on their opponents. To the audience (and inexperienced referees), it often appeared that hits had been scored at the same time, but electronic scoring technology has now made the scoring system much clearer.

Fencers use modified versions of traditional equipment that includes electronic wiring. Each competitor holds a sword and wears a metallic vest (called a lamé) and a body cord. The body cord is a wire that is part of the system for electrically detecting when the weapon has touched the opponent. This body cord connects together electronic sensors in the vest and sword.

When a fencer makes contact with an opponent's lamé, it completes an electrical circuit. Once the circuit is complete, a radio transmitter sends a signal to an electronic scoring machine to tell it that a point has been scored.

THE SCIENCE BEHIND: ELECTRONIC TIMING CHIPS

Traditionally, it was hard to get accurate timings for all competitors at large amateur events, such as marathons. Volunteers with stopwatches and clipboards wrote down times.

Today, events use high-tech timing systems to track entrants. There are three parts to it: a timing chip for each runner (a wrist or ankle band; see picture below), a series of rubber mats containing antennas and radio transmitters, and a computer.

At the race's start, each athlete passes over one of the rubber mats. The antenna inside the mat recognizes the athletes' chips and sends a signal to the computer to begin timing their race. As runners move around the course, they pass over more of these mats, which feed back details of their progress to the computer.

When they pass over the mat on the finish line, a signal is sent to the computer telling it to stop timing. After the race, athletes are given a printout showing their race time and a breakdown of how long it took them to complete each section of the course.

Keeping track of athletes

Today, cutting-edge technology isn't just for the professionals. For example, the electronic timing chip is a technology both amateurs and professionals use.

Technology for all

The widespread use of electronic timing in amateur sports events is just one example of the impact of technology on sports at all levels. Today, technology that was once only available to well-paid professionals is even available to those on a budget.

- Sports equipment made of carbon-fiber composite materials, such as tennis rackets, golf clubs, and bicycles, is now much cheaper and available in popular sporting good stores.
- Sports clothing made from human-made textiles, such as **neoprene** and Lycra, can be bought fairly cheaply from sporting good stores.
- GPS location trackers, which tell you where you go and how fast, are now available as easy-to-use smartphone applications. They can be downloaded for very little money.

Everywhere you look, there are examples of once cutting-edge technology becoming part of the fabric of sports. Clothing, equipment, training methods, and competitions have all felt the impact of technological advancements.

Even the way we watch sports on television has been revolutionized by the march of technology, as we have seen with the examples of ProZone and FIELDf/x. In the 21st century, sports and technology are almost inseparable.

TIMELINE

1901: Sporting goods manufacturer Frank Bryan unveils the first table tennis bat to feature a rubber surface with which to hit the ball. This allows players to put spin on the ball and turns table tennis into an athletic sport.

1913: In Dresden, Germany, the first laboratory for the assessment of athletes and the first sports medicine association are founded. Modern sports medicine is born.

1920: The first international association of sports doctors is founded in St. Moritz, Switzerland, at the Winter Olympic Games.

1939: John T. Riddel invents the first plastic football helmet. However, the use of helmets will not become mandatory for all players until 1943.

1948: The Stoke Mandeville Games take place in London at the same time as the Olympic Games. This is the world's first multisport competition for athletes with disabilities. It will start to include international athletes from 1952. In 1960, it will be renamed the Paralympic Games.

1961: A videotape replay is used for the first time on television, during coverage of a Boston College–Syracuse football game. The replay is aired at half time, many minutes after the point was scored. One of the commentators says that it will "change TV sports forever."

1963: A permanent, artificial "dry" ski slope opens in Torquay, in England. It still exists and is believed to be the world's oldest dry ski slope still in use.

1963: On December 7, CBS airs an "instant replay" of a one-yard scoring run during the Army–Navy football game. This is the world's first use of "instant replay."

1965: Gatorade, the world's first sports drink, goes on sale. It is named after the sports team that first used it: the football team called the Florida Gators.

1967: Wilson Sporting Goods unveils the T2000, the first tennis racket with a full metal frame.

1970: Aluminum bats are introduced to baseball. They will be declared legal for use in Major League Baseball in 1974. The MLB will later ban their use over safety concerns for fielders and spectators.

1975: Danny Litwhiler and John Paulson develop the first baseball radar gun, which measures the speed of pitches, throws, and hits.

1980: Dunlop introduces a tennis racket made of graphite, a composite material. It weighs just 12.5 ounces (354 grams) and becomes popular with professional players.

1986: In response to Uwe Hohn's 1984 javelin world record of 104.8 meters, the International Association of Athletics Federations orders javelins to be redesigned. This makes throws much shorter.

1998: ProZone, a revolutionary system for analyzing soccer matches, goes on sale for the first time.

1999: Lance Armstrong becomes the first Tour de France winner to ride the race on a bike that boasts an all carbon-fiber frame. Later, Armstrong will confess to using illegal performance enhancing drugs to help him secure his successes.

2000: The UCI, the governing body of cycling, decides to change the rules of the Hour Record, the most sought-after in the sport. Cyclists including Chris Boardman and Graham Obree had recently smashed the record using streamlined, high-tech bikes and adapted aerodynamic riding positions. The UCI decides to create two records: the "Athlete Record," for those riding a normal racing bike, and the "Best Human Effort." This category allows riders to use modified bikes and aerodynamic positions.

2001: Mathematician Paul Hawkins invents the HawkEye ball-tracking system, which revolutionizes athletes' and spectators' ability to see where balls truly land. A year later, it is introduced into TV coverage of tennis, allowing players and fans to see if balls were inside or outside the lines of the court.

2011: The Boston Red Sox become the first Major League Baseball team to use the FIELDf/x defensive analysis system.

2013: Goal-line technology is used in soccer's English Premier League for the first time. A year later, it is used at the FIFA World Cup. France's second goal against Honduras becomes the first to be awarded thanks to the technology.

GLOSSARY

adaptation change made to make something more suitable for a new purpose or situation. The body makes adaptations following exercise to enable it to do the same exercise more regularly, at a higher intensity.

amateur person who takes part in an activity—for example, sports—purely for enjoyment

artificial made or produced to seem like something natural

base fitness athlete's underlying fitness level. This is an athlete's starting point, and one he or she will improve on over weeks and months of regular training.

biomechanics study of human movement and the processes in the body that allow movement

blood transfusion adding donated blood to a person's own blood, usually to increase the volume or make it healthier

carbon-fiber composite material made out of carbon woven into long, thin strands. It's usually combined with polymer plastic to create a composite that is used to make sports equipment.

controversy argument that involves many people, often lasting a long time

current steady and continuous flow of water in a particular direction—for example, in a counter-current swimming machine, the machine makes the water flow against the swimmers so they have to work harder

fatigue feeling of extreme tiredness. Fatigue often sets in when a person has been exercising a lot.

friction force of resistance created by two or more objects rubbing together

GPS short for "Global Positioning System." It communicates with satellites that are circling Earth, which then pinpoint the position of a person, car, or cell phone anywhere on the planet.

intensity how hard, fast, or strong something is being performed

isokinetic scientific term for constant speed

manufacturer maker of a particular product—for example, a piece of sports equipment

neoprene type of rubber, created in a laboratory and now used in the manufacture of sports clothing (especially wetsuits)

nutritionist health professional who specializes in advising people on what to eat and drink in order to improve their fitness or lose weight. Many professional athletes employ sports nutritionists to help them with their training.

physical anything relating to the human body, or something that exists in the real world and can be touched (for example, CDs are physical products, while MP3 files are not)

physiotherapist health professional who specializes in human movement. In sports, physiotherapists manage and treat injuries.

professional somebody who does something for a living. Professional athletes are those who are paid to take part in sports.

revolutionary change so dramatic that it changes something forever

sports nutrition science of how food and drink affect exercise and recovery

starting blocks metal block that holds an athlete's feet at the start of a race, so he or she doesn't slip while pushing off after the starter's gun goes off

stimulant food, drink, or supplement that speeds up a bodily process or function

supplement in sports, something that is usually eaten or taken to enhance performance

umpire like a referee; an official who watches over a sport to make sure that the rules of the game are obeyed. Officials in baseball and tennis are known as umpires.

variable something that can change in quality, quantity, and size. You can test how different variables affect the way an experiment turns out.

FIND OUT MORE

Books

Hile, Lori. *Getting Ahead: Drugs, Technology, and Competitive Advantage* (Ethics of Sports). Chicago: Heinemann Library, 2012.

Hunter, Nick. *High-Tech Olympics* (The Olympics). Chicago: Heinemann Library, 2012.

Ross, Stewart. *Sports Technology* (New Technology). Mankato, Minn.: Smart Apple Media, 2012.

Snedden, Robert. *Nutrition: From Birth to Old Age* (Your Body for Life). Chicago: Heinemann Library, 2013.

Web sites

Use FactHound to find Internet sites related to this book. All of the sites on FactHound have been researched by our staff.

Here's all you do:
Visit *www.facthound.com*
Type in this code: 9781484626368

Projects

- Do you have a favorite athlete? Research how he or she keeps in top shape by eating the right things for the kind of sport he or she does as well as the athlete's exercise regimen.
- Examine how sports equipment has changed through time by asking your teachers, parents, or grandparents if they have any old balls, rackets, shoes, or clothing you can take a look at. For example, you could try playing tennis with both wooden and modern composite rackets. You could even go to a local bike store and ask to take a look at the lightest, most expensive carbon-fiber composite bicycles that they have. You'll be amazed how light they are!
- Why not compare the differences in performances between amateur athletes and professional athletes? You could do this by watching games of basketball, baseball, and soccer at your local park, then going to a professional game at a big stadium. Pay close attention to the differences in the speed of players, the quality of play, the tactics, and the way the games are umpired or refereed. If you are lucky, you might also get to see sports technology in action—for example, the use of large video screens to help make refereeing or umpiring decisions.

INDEX